Low-Carb Cocktails

Also by Marlene Koch

Fantastic Food with Splenda: 160 Great Recipes for Meals Low in Sugar, Carbohydrates, Fat, and Calories

Unbelievable Desserts with Splenda: Sweet Treats Low in Sugar, Fat, and Calories

50 Splenda Recipes: Favorites from Fantastic Food with Splenda and Unbelievable Desserts with Splenda

Low-Carb Cocktails

All the Fun and Taste Without the Carbs

Marlene and Chuck Koch

illustrations by Christopher Dollbaum

M. Evans and Company, Inc.
New York

M. Evans and Company, Inc.
216 East 49th Street
New York, NY 10017

This book offers beverages that should be enjoyed as part of an overall healthy diet and is not intended as a dietary prescription. Persons with health concerns should seek the advice of a qualified professional, such as a physician or registered dietitian, for a personalized diet plan. Even though the FDA has determined sucralose to be safe for everyone, persons consuming Splenda do so at their own risk. Neither the authors nor the publisher is liable for the product and neither is in any way affiliated with the manufacturer, McNeil Specialty Products

Splenda is a registered trademark of McNeil Specialty Products Company, a Division of McNeil-PPc Inc.

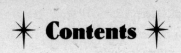

✳ **Contents** ✳

We dedicate this book to our family, friends, and neighbors, who have shared good times, wonderful food, and fabulous libations with us over the years. You have inspired us in countless ways to create and continually explore new and exciting ways to entertain you—and, thus, ourselves. Saluté!

✳ **Introduction** ✳

Celebrating with a cocktail is a wonderful part of life, but if your lifestyle includes watching your carbs, this can create quite a dilemma. But worry no more, that conflict no longer exists, because we have made it possible for you to enjoy many of your favorite libations, both alcoholic and nonalcoholic, while still living your low-carb lifestyle.

We developed the recipes in this book because we, like you, didn't want to give up the occasional cocktail, pass on enjoying the wonderfully delicious specialty drinks that are the current rage, or give up enjoying eggnog and other festive drinks during the holidays. So, out of necessity, we have developed great-tasting low-carb cocktails that range from classics like the Perfect Manhattan to bar favorites like the Margaritas and Long Island Iced Tea. For lazing by the pool, there is a cool and creamy Piña Colada, and for holiday parties, a Killer Eggnog. In addition, you'll also enjoy luscious novelty drinks like the ultrahip Lemon Drop and our original fruity creation called the Chuck Wagon. We're confident that with the more than 60 cocktails in this book, including amazing recipes for low-carb Coffee Liqueur (Mock Kahlua) and Orange Liqueur (Mock Grand Marnier), as well as suggestions for nonalcoholic versions of some of them, you'll definitely be ready to serve great-tasting drinks to all your friends (and yourself) for every occasion.

Last, but not least, not only have all the recipes been professionally analyzed, but you will also find a chapter on Carbohydrates and Alcohol that will help you understand how cocktails can fit into your low-carb diet, as well as a chapter on Cocktail Basics that includes ingredients to help you create "all the taste without the carbs" cocktails.

Cheers! (and remember to drink responsibly)

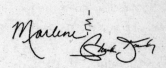

Part One

Carbohydrates
and
Alcohol

Carbohydrates and Alcohol 101

The good news is that most straight alcohol spirits have little or no carbs! Alcohol does not metabolize as carbohydrate (to produce sugar), nor does it metabolize as a protein or fat. Technically speaking, alcohol is in a class by itself. But, on the other hand, alcohol is metabolized exclusively for energy and provides 7 calories per gram as a readily available fuel source (meaning that your body will use it for energy before using your stored fat). It's for this reason that many low-carb diets restrict the drinking of alcohol in the initial, or induction, phase. Once you're beyond that dieting phase (or if you're watching your weight by simply restricting your carb intake), drinking alcoholic beverages in moderation should present no problem as long as you keep track of the carbs. We know this sounds easy, but it's not as easy as you think when you start trying to add up the carbs in the alcohol with those additional calories found in the sugary mixers, liqueurs, and juices that often make up a cocktail. But we're here to do all that for you. Not only have we creatively curbed these "extra carbs" so you can enjoy our delicious drinks as part of your low-carb lifestyle, but we've conveniently included the total number of carbs for each recipe so you can easily keep within the guidelines of your particular diet.

Alcohol, Carbs, and Calories

The following chart is included to help you understand which types of alcohol contain the most carbohydrates and calories. This information will help you stay within your daily carb or calorie count when drinking straight liquors, wine, or beer or developing your own recipes. The following chart shows that distilled spirits like gin and vodka have no carbohydrates, but they do have calories. Wine has only 1 to 2 grams of carb per serving, followed by light beers, which currently range from as low as a mere 2.6 grams to as high as 6.7 grams per bottle. On the other end of the alcohol spectrum, note the high number of carbs in sweet wines and commercially produced sugary, syrupy liqueurs.

CARBOHYDRATES AND CALORIES IN COMMON ALCOHOLIC BEVERAGES

DRINK	Carbohydrates (Grams)	Calories
BEER (12 OUNCES)		
Regular	13	150
Light	2.6 – 6.7	90 –100
LIQUEURS (1 OUNCE)		
Amaretto	16	110
Bailey's Irish Cream	7.5	115
Grand Marnier	6.5	75
Mock Grand Marnier (page 68)	3	70
Kahlua	14	60
Mock Kahlua (page 59)	2	45
Triple Sec	11	100
SPIRITS (1 OUNCE, 80 PROOF)*		
Bourbon	0	65
Brandy	trace	65
Cognac	0	65
Rum	0	65
Scotch	0	65
Tequila	0	65
Vodka	0	65
Whiskey	0	65
WINE (4 OUNCES)*		
Champagne, brut	4	90
Champagne, rose	8	100
Red, dry	2	90
White, dry	1	80
White, sweet dessert	12	150

*Carbohydrates vary by producer. These are averages.

✴ **Part Two** ✴

Cocktail Basics

Ingredients

In order to make the great-tasting cocktails in this book, you need to use the proper ingredients. For example, if we recommend using a name-brand liquor and you use a house brand, the taste might not be as good as you would like. Likewise, if you want to substitute flavored liqueurs for extracts or use more fruit juice than we specify, this will add more carbohydrate to the finished product. Furthermore, don't skimp on the garnish, because in many cases, it will affect more than the look of the drink. Here are some more tips to help you select and prepare the ingredients for consistently perfect cocktails:

Distilled spirits are the basic alcohols—gin, vodka, rum, tequila, etc. Changing just the spirit will create a whole new drink. We suggest that you use not only high-quality spirits, but pay attention to brand names when they are mentioned in a recipe, because they can make a distinguishable taste difference in the final drink. Also note that we've used pre-flavored liquors such as orange and citrus vodka instead of sugar-laden liqueurs. These flavored spirits are a great way to add flavor to drinks without adding carbs.

Extracts also add flavor without carbs. You'll notice that we make great use of natural extracts like vanilla, orange, and lemon, which are easily found in the baking section of any supermarket.

Fresh fruits, especially berries, are fabulous for their flavor and scent. The ones we've selected have only 3 to 5 grams of net carb per $\frac{1}{2}$ cup of fruit.

Fruit juices are usually high in carbs, so we have minimized their use. The exceptions to this rule are lemon juice and lime juice. Fresh squeezed is best, but the bottled varieties are fine. (Do not use Rose's lime juice—it is sweetened.)

Garnishes are used to enhance taste, scent, and eye appeal.

* A citrus twist is easily made by using a zester or small paring knife to remove a long strip of just the peel of the fruit (including some of the white pith to keep the twist sturdy).

* A slice is a half circle of fruit with its peel and is used mostly to decorate the rim of the glass. A wedge of fruit means that the juice of the fruit is to be squeezed into the cocktail before drinking.

* Fresh mint, olives (which are very low in carbs), and maraschino cherries (which contain only 1 gram of carbohydrate per cherry) add taste and decoration to a variety of drinks.

Ice needs to be clean and odor-free. For this reason, commercially bagged ice is often best. When a recipe calls for crushed ice and you have cubes, place a few in a plastic bag and crush them with a mallet. If the drink is to be mixed in a blender, whole cubes can be used, but they will take longer to blend.

Liqueurs are notoriously high in sugar and are used sparingly. We use Grand Marnier specifically for orange liqueur because it has the lowest carb content of all the orange liqueurs. You can also make your own with our recipe (page 68) and save an *additional* 2 grams of carb per ½ ounce. All drinks that call for coffee liqueur use our low-carb version (page 59). Regular coffee liqueurs are far too high in carbohydrate.

Splenda is used in place of sugar. Splenda is a noncaloric sugar substitute that is made from sugar. Recipes call for Splenda Granular, found (in a yellow box) next to the sugar in most supermarkets. If you use Splenda packets, note that each packet equals 2 teaspoons of Splenda Granular.

Sugar-free syrups and mixers are now widely available and can be found in the liquor or low-carb section of supermarkets, at low-carb specialty stores, and on the Web. Toriani and DaVinci are two good brands of sugar-free syrups, and Baja Bob's makes a good low-carb sweet-and-sour mix.

Tools of the Trade

There are many fancy bar tools you can buy, but these few basics are all you truly need.

* Blender
* Corkscrew
* Cutting board
* Juice squeezer
* Bottle pourers
* Shaker—stainless steel or glass (*not* aluminum)
* Shot glass
* Strainer
* Zester

Mixing Techniques

There are three ways to mix drinks: shaking, stirring, and muddling:

Shaking ensures a thorough mixing of heavy or cloudy ingredients like juices, cream, or eggs. Shaking also produces piercingly cold strained cocktails when done with clear ingredients. Drinks should be shaken vigorously for 10 to 20 seconds—long enough for the outside of the shaker to feel cold, but not so long that the drink becomes diluted by the ice.

Stirring is the technique that is used mostly with clear or light ingredients or when complete mixing is not essential. The idea behind stirring is not only to mix the ingredients but to cool them and dilute them with a bit of melted ice. Stirring should be done for about 20 seconds.

Muddling is a less common mixing technique, but it's essential for releasing the oils and juices from fruit or, in the case of the Mojito, mint leaves. You can buy a muddler or you can use the back of a spoon to press the ingredient against the side of an empty glass before adding the rest of the drink's contents.

Measures

The ingredients for the cocktails in this book are measured in ounces. The easiest and most accurate way to do this is to get yourself a 1-ounce shot glass or a jigger. Beware, however, because jiggers come in 1 and $1^1/_2$ ounce sizes, and one particularly popular version, called a double-sided jigger, combines both sizes in one measure. The larger-quantity drinks are measured in cups, so you'll also need a glass 1-cup measure.

The following equivalents will help you measure accurately.

3 teaspoons = 1 tablespoon
½ ounce = 1 tablespoon
1 ounce = 2 tablespoons
1½ ounces = 1 jigger
2 ounces = ¼ cup
8 ounces = 1 cup
16 ounces = 1 pint
750 milliliters = 25.4 ounces
1 fifth = 25.6 ounces
1 quart = 32 ounces

Glassware

We have specified specific glassware on all the recipes, but these are just guidelines. If you don't have a particular glass, don't worry, just use something that is similar in size (you don't want the glass to look half empty) and transparent if you'd like the drink to show through. Keep in mind, though, that using the right glassware for a particular cocktail not only looks good, but is done for a purpose. For example, stemmed glasses are used so your hand doesn't warm the drink, whereas a brandy snifter is designed to be held in the palm of your hand so that it *does* warm the liquor. More important, however, is that you pay particular attention to chilling the glass when the recipe calls for it.

Chilling the glass. There two simple ways to accomplish this.

1. Place the glass or glasses in the refrigerator or freezer (10 minutes will do). However, do not chill very fine crystal in the freezer—it may crack.
2. A quicker way is to fill the glass with ice and cold water and place it in or near a sink while you make your drink. Swirl the ice around the glass and pour it out before you add the drink, and be careful to shake out all excess water.

Cocktail Glassware

Rocks   Highball   Tom Collins

Wine Glass   Wine Goblet   Champagne Flute

Glass Coffee Mug   Cocktail (Martini)   Margarita

✳ Cocktail Recipes ✳

Classics

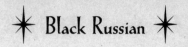

✳ Black Russian ✳

We like to think of this drink as "espresso with a kick." Homemade sugar-free coffee liqueur is the trick to cutting the carbs.

Net Carbs 2

1   ounce vodka
1   ounce coffee liqueur
    (page 59)

Fill rocks glass with ice. Pour in vodka and coffee liqueur. Stir.

Calories 110

Variation: Mocha Russian—add 1 ounce sugar-free chocolate-flavored syrup (like DaVinci or Torani) before stirring.

✳ Chuck's Classic Martini ✳

Every step and ingredient counts when making a truly great martini. Having everything ready, including a martini glass chilling in the freezer, will give you the professional edge.

Net Carbs 0

> ⅛   teaspoon Cointreau or Grand Marnier
> 3   ounces Ketel One or other high-quality vodka
> Lemon twist or green olive

Swirl Cointreau or Grand Marnier to coat inside of a well-chilled martini glass. Shake out any excess. Set aside. Pour vodka in a shaker ⅔ full of ice. Shake very well and strain into prepared glass. Rim lemon twist around edge of glass and drop in, or add olive. *Serve piercingly cold.*

Calories 195

Variation: Gin Martini—substitute 3 ounces high-quality gin for vodka.

✷ Dirty Martini ✷

Olives are full of flavor yet wonderfully low in carbohydrate. This rustic martini provides the perfect prelude to a good steak.

Net Carbs 1

3	ounces vodka (or gin)
½	ounce olive juice
¼	ounce dry vermouth (optional)
2	green pimento-stuffed olives

Pour vodka (or gin), olive juice, and vermouth into a shaker ⅔ full of ice. Shake well. Strain into chilled martini glass. Add olives.

Calories 205

✶ Mint Julep ✶

Net Carbs 1

Mint Juleps made with Kentucky bourbon are *the official drink* of the Kentucky Derby. If you're not at the derby, any bourbon will do. Giddyup!

> **Fresh mint leaves**
> 2 teaspoons Splenda Granular
> 2 tablespoons water
> 2½ ounces bourbon
> **Splash of club soda**

In a large rocks glass, using the back of a spoon, press and crush 5 to 8 mint leaves (to break apart and release oils) with Splenda and water. Fill glass with ice. Add bourbon and stir. Top with club soda and garnish with additional mint leaves.

Calories 170

✳ Old-Fashioned ✳

To make a good Old-Fashioned, you need to use the bartending technique called "muddling," which uses the back of a spoon (or muddler) to break up the fruit and release its juices and oils to flavor the liquid (see page 13).

Net Carbs 3

- 2   dashes Angostura bitters
- 1   teaspoon Splenda Granular
- 1   orange slice (thin)
- 2   lemon twists
- 1   maraschino cherry
- 2   ounces bourbon (or blended Canadian whiskey)

Splash of club soda

Lemon twist

In a large rocks glass, muddle the bitters, Splenda, orange slice, lemon twists, and maraschino cherry. Fill the glass with ice. Add bourbon and a splash of club soda. Stir. Garnish with lemon twist.

Calories 135

✴ Perfect Manhattan ✴

Equal parts of sweet and dry vermouth make this a "perfect" Manhattan.

Net Carbs 5

2 ounces bourbon (V.O. or blended Canadian whiskey)
1 ounce sweet vermouth
1 ounce dry vermouth
2 dashes angostura bitters
Lemon Twist or maraschino cherry*

Pour bourbon, sweet and dry vermouth, and bitters into a shaker ¾ full of ice. Shake well. Strain into chilled martini glass. Add lemon twist or cherry.

Calories 210

Variation: Rob Roy—substitute scotch for bourbon.
*Add 1 carb gram if cherry garnish is used (and eaten!)

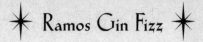

✦ Ramos Gin Fizz ✦

This classic cocktail takes a full 3 minutes of shaking—but it's worth every minute!

Net Carbs 4

>   2   ounces gin
>   2   teaspoons lemon juice
>   1   teaspoon lime juice
>   1   tablespoon Splenda
>   Granular
>   1   tablespoon light cream
>   1   large egg white
> Dash (or ⅛ teaspoon) orange
>   extract
> 2½ ounces club soda

Combine all ingredients except club soda in a shaker filled ¾ full of ice, and shake for 3 minutes. Strain into chilled wine goblet. Add club soda and stir briefly.

Calories 185

✳ Side Car ✳

This classic dates back to WWI. It is reportedly named for a customer who ordered it at his favorite Parisian bar, which he was driven to in the sidecar of a motorcycle.

Net Carbs 5

> **2** ounces cognac
> **½** ounce Grand Marnier
> **½** ounce fresh lemon juice
> **1** teaspoon Splenda Granular
> **Lemon twist**

Pour all ingredients except lemon twist into a shaker ¾ full of ice. Shake well. Rim the edge of a chilled cocktail. glass with lemon twist. Strain drink into glass. Add twist.

Calories 170

✳ Ultra-Low-Carb Side Car ✳

This ultra-low-carb version of our Side Car substitutes vodka, orange extract, and Splenda for the Grand Marnier.

Net Carbs 2

- 2 ounces cognac
- ½ ounce vodka
- ⅛ teaspoon orange extract
- 1½ teaspoons Splenda Granular
- ½ ounce fresh lemon juice
- Lemon twist

Pour all ingredients except lemon twist into a shaker ¾ full of ice. Shake well. Rim the edge of a chilled cocktail glass with lemon twist. Strain drink into glass. Add twist.

Calories 150

✳ Tom Collins ✳

An old English classic, so-named because it was originally made with "Old Tom," a sweetened gin.

Net Carbs 3

> **2 ounces gin**
> **1 ounce lemon juice**
> **1 teaspoon Splenda Granular**
> **4 ounces club soda**
> **1 orange twist**

In a tall collins glass, combine gin, lemon juice, and Splenda. Stir. Fill glass with ice and top with club soda. Garnish with orange twist.

Calories 140

Variation: John Collins—substitute diet ginger ale for club soda.

✳ Whiskey Sour ✳

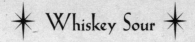

Net Carbs 1

Traditional sweet-and-sour mixers are very high in sugar. To make this, use one of the new low-carb versions now available at liquor stores or low-carb retailers.

2 **ounces bourbon (or blend-ed Canadian whiskey)**
½ **ounce lemon juice**
½ **ounce low-carb sweet-and-sour mix (like Baja Bob's)**
Lemon twist

Pour bourbon, lemon juice, and sweet-and-sour mix into a shaker ⅔ full of ice. Shake well. Pour into rocks glass filled with ice. Garnish with lemon twist.

Calories 135

✴ White Russian ✴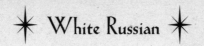

A creamy, rich, and smooth cousin of the Black Russian—yum!

Net Carbs 3

> 1 **ounce vodka**
> 1 **ounce coffee liqueur (page 59)**
> 1 **ounce light cream**
> **Squirt light sweetened whipped cream (optional)***

Fill rocks glass with ice. Pour in vodka, coffee liqueur, and cream. Stir to swirl. Top with whipped cream if desired.

Calories 165

*Add 1 gram carbs if whipped cream is used.

✳ Cocktail Recipes ✳

Bar Favorites

✳ Bloody Mary ✳

Rich in antioxidants and with only 1 gram of carbohydrate per ounce, tomato juice just can't be beat—unless you spruce it up with spice and vodka to make this great brunch favorite.

Net Carbs 7

2 **ounces vodka**
4 **ounces tomato juice**
½ **ounce lemon juice**
½ **teaspoon horseradish**
2 dashes Worcestershire sauce
1 or 2 dashes Tabasco sauce
¼ **teaspoon black pepper**
¼ **teaspoon celery salt**
Celery stalk
Small lemon wedge

Fill highball glass with ice. Add all ingredients except celery stalk and lemon wedge. Stir briskly. Add celery stalk and garnish edge with lemon wedge.

Calories 160

Variation: Bloody Eight—use V8 as a substitute for tomato juice. Nonalcoholic variation: Virgin Mary—omit vodka.

✦ Brandy Alexander ✦

Dessert in a glass! Chocolate, cream, and brandy. Yum, yum, yum.

Net Carbs 1

2   ounces brandy
1   ounce sugar-free chocolate syrup (like DaVinci's or Torani's)
1   ounce light cream
Sprinkle of freshly ground nutmeg (optional)

Pour brandy, chocolate syrup, and cream in a shaker ⅔ full of ice. Shake well. Strain into chilled cocktail glass. Garnish with nutmeg if desired.

Calories 190

✳ Gin and Tonic ✳

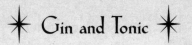

By simply substituting sugar-free tonic in this popular cocktail, you can save up to 15 grams of carbohydrate per drink.

Net Carbs 1

> 1½ **ounces gin**
> 5 **ounces sugar-free (diet) tonic water**
> 1 **lime wedge**

Fill tall collins glass with ice. Pour in gin and tonic. Stir. Squeeze lime wedge and drop it into the drink.

Calories 100

Variation: Vodka Tonic—substitute vodka for gin.

✳ Irish Coffee ✳

Irish whiskey is essential for this belly-warming drink that has made the Buena Vista in San Francisco world renowned.

Net Carbs 3

> 1½ ounces Irish whiskey
> 2 teaspoons Splenda Granular
> 5 ounces fresh brewed coffee
> 1 squirt light whipped cream

Stir together the Irish whiskey and Splenda in an Irish coffee glass (glass coffee mug or wine glass). Add coffee. Stir. Top with whipped cream.

Calories 125

✦ Kamikaze ✦

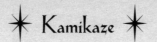

This grown-up Kamikaze is served elegantly in a chilled cocktail glass (but still carries the same old kick).

Net Carbs 4

>   2   **ounces vodka**
>   1   **ounce lime juice**
>   1   **tablespoon Splenda**
>   **Granular**
>   **Slice of lime**

Pour vodka, lime juice, and Splenda into a shaker ¾ full of ice. Shake well. Rim the edge of a chilled cocktail glass with lime. Strain drink into glass. Garnish edge with lime.

Calories 140

✳ Long Island Ice Tea ✳

No section on bar favorites would be complete without this party-bar staple. It's an amazing concoction that allows this mixture of spirits to taste simply like iced tea. Watch out!

Net Carbs 2

- ½ **ounce vodka**
- ½ **ounce light rum**
- ½ **ounce gin**
- ¼ **ounce light tequila**
- ½ **ounce lemon juice**
- 1 **teaspoon Splenda Granular**
- **Splash of diet cola**
- **Lemon wedge**

Fill a highball glass with ice. Pour in all ingredients except diet cola and lemon wedge. Stir. Add diet cola and stir lightly. Garnish edge with lemon.

Calories 130

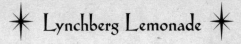

✦ Lynchberg Lemonade ✦

The T.G.I.F. restaurant chain serves up this sweet touch of Southern hospitality (along with over 10 times the carbs!) in a large goblet, with a straw of to match.

Net Carbs 3

2	ounces Jack Daniel's
½	ounce vodka
1	ounce lemon juice
2	teaspoons Splenda Granular
⅛	teaspoon orange extract
3	ounces diet lemon-lime soda (Sprite or 7-Up)

Lemon slice

Fill a tall collins glass with ice. Pour all ingredients except soda and lemon slice into glass. Stir. Add soda and stir lightly. Garnish edge with lemon slice.

Calories 170

✦ Margarita ✦

Sipping this drink of Mexico has definitely become an American pastime. Without the sugary mixers, this favorite plummets from over 25 grams of carbohydrate to just 7 grams per serving.

Net Carbs 7

- 2 **ounces tequila**
- ½ **ounce Grand Marnier**
- 1 **ounce lime juice**
- 2 **teaspoons Splenda Granular**
- **Lime wedge (optional)**
- **Coarse salt (optional)**

Pour tequila, Grand Marnier, lime juice, and Splenda into a shaker ⅔ full of ice. Shake well. Rim the edge of an ice-filled rocks glass with lime. If desired, wet the rim of the glass with the lime wedge and dip rim into salt. Strain drink into glass.

Calories 165

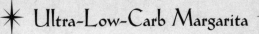

✳ Ultra-Low-Carb Margarita ✳

You can buy powdered low-carb margarita mix, but since we prefer the taste
of real lime juice, we created this margarita for those with really strict carb
limits.

Net
Carbs
4

2½ ounces tequila
1 ounce lime juice
⅛ teaspoon orange extract
1 tablespoon Splenda
Granular
Lime wedge (optional)
Coarse salt (optional)

Pour tequila, lime juice, orange extract, and Splenda
into a shaker ⅔ full of ice. Shake well. Rim the edge of
an ice-filled rocks glass with lime. If desired, wet the
rim of the glass with the lime wedge and dip rim into
salt. Strain drink into glass.

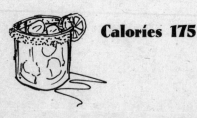

Calories 175

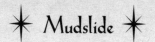

✳ Mudslide ✳

Like a milkshake—only better! Low-carb ice cream helps to drastically slash the carbs in this rich and filling treat. We particularly like Breyer's brand, with only 4 grams net carb per serving.

Net Carbs 7

- 1 ounce vodka
- 1 ounce coffee liqueur (page 59)
- 1 ounce light cream
- ½ ounce Irish whiskey
- ½ ounce sugar-free chocolate syrup (optional)
- ½ cup low-carb chocolate ice cream
- ¾ cup crushed ice

Pour all ingredients except ice cream and ice into a blender. Add ice cream and blend until smooth. Add crushed ice and blend on high until cold and creamy. Pour into a large wine goblet.

Calories 330

✷ Strawberry Margarita ✷

Nothing says summer like a big Strawberry Margarita by the pool. Frozen
berries work best to impart the right
texture to this drink, so if you use fresh
berries, clean, stem, and freeze them first.

Net Carbs 7

3	ounces gold tequila
½	ounce lime juice
1½	tablespoons Splenda Granular
⅛	teaspoon orange extract
4	whole frozen strawberries
¾	cup crushed ice

Pour all ingredients except strawberries and ice into
blender. Add strawberries and blend until smooth.
Add crushed ice and blend on high until cold and
frosty. Pour into a large margarita glass.

Calories 220

✳ Wine Spritzer ✳

A refreshing drink with a nice touch of citrus for those times when you prefer a light drink.

Net Carbs 1

    4   ounces white wine
    2   ounces club soda
    Lemon twist

Fill an 8-ounce wineglass with ice. Pour in wine and soda. Stir briefly and add lemon twist.

Calories 80

✳ Cocktail Recipes ✳

Tropical Libations

✳ Chuck's Tropical Punch ✳

This recipe is for one, but you can multiply it as many times as you need to serve a crowd. (In fact, multiplying it by four makes one heck of a party for two!)

Net Carbs 6

1   ounce each white rum and gold rum
½   ounce Grand Marnier (or orange liqueur, page 68)
½   ounce brandy
½   ounce lime juice
½   ounce pineapple juice
½   ounce low-carb sweet-and-sour mix (like Baja Bob's)
Splash of club soda
½   orange slice

In a tall rocks glass, combine all ingredients except club soda and orange slice. Stir. Fill glass with ice, top with club soda, and stir lightly. Garnish with orange slice.

Calories 200

✳ Coconut Creamsicle ✳

Coconut milk adds a tropical flair to this big and refreshing 12-ounce drink reminiscent of the frozen orange sherbet and vanilla ice cream treat for which this is named.

Net Carbs 3

- 3 ounces coconut milk (may substitute light coconut milk)
- 2 ounces vodka
- 1 tablespoon Splenda Granular
- ½ teaspoon vanilla extract
- ¼ teaspoon orange extract
- 1 large egg white
- 1 cup crushed ice

Orange twist

Pour all ingredients except orange twist into blender. Blend on high until smooth and creamy. Pour into a wine goblet. Garnish with orange twist.

Calories 320

Variation: Nonalcoholic version—substitute 1 ounce each of heavy cream and water for vodka (net carbs 5).

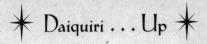

✳ Daiquiri . . . Up ✳

We prefer our daiquiris "up" (with no ice), as they were originally served in the 1800s. If you prefer, you may strain the cocktail into an ice-filled rocks glass.

> 2 **ounces white rum**
> 1 **ounce lime juice**
> 2 **teaspoons Splenda Granular**
> **Lime twist**

Pour all ingredients into a shaker ⅔ full of ice. Shake well. Strain into chilled cocktail glass. Garnish with lime twist.

Calories 140

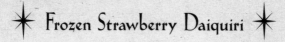

✳ Frozen Strawberry Daiquiri ✳

Net
Carbs
7

It's hard to believe this fruity and luscious drink isn't high in carbs, especially when it tastes just like the traditional bar version, which can easily contain
40 grams of carbs or more. Enjoy.

3   ounces light rum
½   ounce lime juice
2   tablespoons Splenda
     Granular
4   whole frozen strawberries
½   cup crushed ice

Place all ingredients except ice into blender. Blend
until smooth. Add crushed ice and blend again on
high until smooth and thick. Pour into a large cocktail
glass.

Calories 220

✴ Lemon Raspberry Slush ✴

A touch less alcohol than our Strawberry Daiquiri, but full of fresh lemon and raspberries, this cold and frosty libation is perfect on a hot day.

Net Carbs 6

1½ ounces Citron vodka
1   ounce lemon juice
2   tablespoons Splenda Granular
½   teaspoon lemon zest
¼   cup fresh raspberries
1   cup crushed ice
Lemon twist

Put all ingredients except ice and lemon twist into blender. Bend until smooth. Add crushed ice and blend again on high until smooth and frosty. Pour into a large rocks glass. Garnish with lemon twist and a straw.

Calories 130

Variation: Nonalcoholic version—substitute ½ ounce lemon juice and 1 ounce water for vodka.

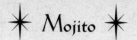

✴ Mojito ✴

Cuban "mo-HEE-toes" are the perfect summertime (okay, anytime) sippers. The fresher the mint, the better the drink.

Net Carbs 4

    Fresh mint leaves
1   ounce fresh lime juice
4   teaspoons Splenda
       Granular
2   ounces white rum
Splash of club soda
Slice of lime (optional)

In a tall collins glass, using the back of a spoon, press and crush 8 to 10 mint leaves (to break apart and release oils) with lime and Splenda. Fill glass with crushed ice. Add rum and top off with club soda. Garnish with slice of lime and/or additional fresh mint.

Calories 155

✦ Piña Colada ✦

This tropical favorite has been called paradise in a glass. Our version has a fraction of the carbs of the standard bar version, with the creamy, sweet pineapple-coconut flavor you love (which is missing from the low-carb mixes). Now this is true paradise.

Net Carbs 8

- 2 ounces rum
- 2 ounces half-and-half
- 1 ounce unsweetened pineapple juice
- 1 tablespoon Splenda
- ½ teaspoon coconut extract
- 1 cup crushed ice

Pour all ingredients except ice into blender. Blend until smooth. Add crushed ice and blend on high until smooth and frosty. Pour into a large rocks glass or wine goblet. Add umbrella if desired!

Calories 230

✦ Ultra-Low-Carb Piña Colada ✦

Substituting pineapple extract for the juice lowers the carbs even more here. Can paradise get any better than this?

Net Carbs 6

2	ounces rum
2	ounces half-and-half
2	tablespoons Splenda Granular
½	teaspoon coconut extract
¼	teaspoon pineapple extract
1	cup crushed ice

Pour all ingredients except ice into blender. Blend until smooth. Add crushed ice and blend on high until smooth and frosty. Pour into a large rocks glass or wine goblet.

Calories 210

✴ Planter's Punch ✴

This traditional island favorite uses part dark rum, but you may use all golden rum if you prefer a milder rum flavor.

Net Carbs 5

1   ounce dark rum
1   ounce golden rum
1   ounce pineapple juice
1   ounce low-carb sweet-and-sour mix (like Baja Bob's)
1   maraschino cherry
1   ounce club soda (optional)
Orange twist

In a tall rocks glass, combine all ingredients except club soda and orange twist. Stir. Fill glass with ice. Top with club soda if desired and stir lightly. Garnish with orange twist.

Calories 160

✦ Rum Punch ✦

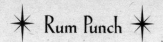

This tastes similar to canned Hawaiian Punch, only with *way* less sugar and, of course, *way* more "punch." For entertaining, make it in a punch bowl by simply multiplying this recipe as many times as you need to fill your punch bowl. Garnish with floating orange slices. (If you increase this recipe, remember that 1 ounce equals 2 tablespoons, and 4 tablespoons equals ¼ cup.)

Net Carbs 6

> 1½ ounces light rum
> 1½ ounces light cranberry juice
> ½ ounce orange juice
> ½ ounce pineapple juice
> ½ teaspoon Splenda Granular
> Orange slice

Pour all ingredients except orange slice into a small rocks glass. Stir, and fill with ice. Garnish with orange slice.

Calories 120

Variation: Nonalcoholic version—substitute ½ ounce additional light cranberry juice and 1 ounce water for rum (adds 1 carb per serving).

✳ Cocktail Recipes ✳

Party Time

✳ Champagne Cocktail ✳

Six ounces of champagne contains approximately 6 grams of carbohydrate—the same as some low-carb beers. Isn't it nice to know you can still celebrate while watching your carbs?

Net Carbs 6

1 teaspoon Splenda Granular

3 dashes Angostura bitters

6 ounces champagne

Place Splenda and bitters in the bottom of a champagne glass. Add champagne. Say "cheers."

Calories 150

✴ Coffee Liqueur ✴
(Mock Kahlua)

This amazing recipe tastes as good as the commercial brand Kahlua, except it costs less and has a fraction of the carbs (2 grams net carbs per ounce versus 14 grams). It's also incredibly versatile for drinks (and more) and makes a great gift.

Net Carbs 2

2 cups hot water
3 cups Splenda Granular
½ cup instant coffee
1 tablespoon good vanilla
(or 1 vanilla bean*)
1 bottle (750 milliliters) vodka

Place hot water into a medium pitcher. Add Splenda and instant coffee and stir to dissolve. Add vanilla and vodka. Stir. Keep in a covered container or pour through a funnel into decorative bottles. Keeps indefinitely. *Makes approximately 1.5 liters, or 46 1-ounce servings.*

Calories 45

*If using vanilla bean, split lengthwise, scrape out seeds, and place into container or bottle before adding coffee mixture.

✳ Eggnog ✳

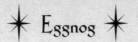

What's a holiday party without eggnog? Here is our favorite nog recipe, made with a blend of milk and cream, along with a nonalcoholic variation for all your guests to enjoy. Ho, ho, ho!

Net Carbs 6

6	egg yolks
¾	cup Splenda Granular
1½	cups heavy cream
2	cups whole milk*
1	tablespoon vanilla
¾	teaspoon nutmeg
¾	cup rum (may also use brandy or cognac)

Additional nutmeg for garnish

In a small bowl, beat egg yolks with electric mixer until light and lemon colored. Beat in Splenda. Slowly beat in 1 cup cream (small amounts at a time to keep in creamy) and then 1 cup milk. Pour into a medium saucepan and cook over low heat, whisking constantly, until mixture is thick enough to coat the back of a spoon. Remove from heat. Stir in vanilla, nutmeg, 1 cup milk, and rum. Refrigerate. Before serving, softly whip remaining ½ cup cream. Whisk into cold eggnog. Ladle into cups and garnish with a sprinkle of nutmeg. *Makes 8 servings.*

Calories 285

Variation: Non-alcoholic variation—substitute ½ to ¾ cup water mixed with 1 teaspoon rum extract for rum.

*Low-carb milk such as Hood brand Carb Countdown may be used, and will reduce net carbs to 4 grams per serving.

✴ Ultra-Low-Carb Killer Eggnog ✴

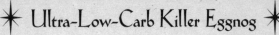

Decadent and rich, this all-cream eggnog is for those of you looking for the maximum carb cut. (Did you know that preprepared eggnogs can contain up to 20 carb grams of per serving?)

Net Carbs 4

6	egg yolks
¾	cup Splenda Granular
2½	cups heavy cream
1	cup water
1	tablespoon vanilla
¾	teaspoon nutmeg
¾	cup rum (may also use brandy or cognac)

Additional nutmeg for garnish

In a small bowl, beat egg yolks with electric mixer until light and lemon colored. Beat in Splenda. Slowly beat in 1 cup cream (small amounts at a time to keep in creamy) and then 1 cup water. Pour into a medium saucepan and cook over low heat, whisking constantly, until mixture is thick enough to coat the back of a spoon. Remove from heat. Stir in vanilla, nutmeg, 1 cup cream, and rum. Refrigerate. Before serving, softly whip remaining ½ cup cream. Whisk into cold eggnog. Ladle into cups and garnish with a sprinkle of nutmeg. *Makes 8 servings.*

Calories 365

✴ Fourth of July Lemonade ✴

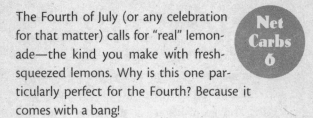

The Fourth of July (or any celebration for that matter) calls for "real" lemonade—the kind you make with fresh-squeezed lemons. Why is this one particularly perfect for the Fourth? Because it comes with a bang!

Net Carbs 6

> 1 cup fresh-squeezed lemon juice
> 1 cup vodka
> 2 cups water
> ⅓ cup Splenda Granular
> 1 tablespoon lemon zest

Pour lemon juice into a large pitcher. Add vodka, water, Splenda, and lemon zest. Stir. Serve over ice. *Makes 5 servings (1 quart).*

Calories 210

Variation: Nonalcoholic version—substitute 1 additional cup of water in place of vodka.

✴ Hot Buttered Rum ✴

Buttery and fragrant with spice, nothing welcomes guests or wards off a cold-weather chill like a steaming mug of Hot Buttered Rum. The butter mixture will keep for several months in the refrigerator.

Net Carbs 4

½ **cup (1 stick) butter, softened**
1   **cup Splenda Granular**
1   **teaspoon molasses**
1   **teaspoon cinnamon**
¾ **teaspoon nutmeg**
½ **teaspoon mace**
Dark rum

Place butter in a food processor. Add Splenda, molasses, and spices and process just until smooth. Scrape butter mixture into a covered container and placed in refrigerator. For each drink, measure 1 ample tablespoon of butter mixture into a mug. Add 5 ounces of boiling water and 1½ ounces of dark rum. Stir briskly. *Makes 8 servings.*

Calories 220

Variation: Nonalcoholic variation—substitute 1 ounce of water and ½ teaspoon rum-flavored extract for dark rum.

✳ Marlene's Moose Milk ✳

I just had to decarb this long-standing family favorite. It's a great brunch tradition (although no one knows where it got this name).

Net Carbs 6

- ½ **cup lemon juice**
- 2 **teaspoons lemon extract**
- ½ **cup Splenda Granular**
- ½ **cup half-and-half**
- ½ **cup vodka**
- 3 **cups crushed ice**

Pour all ingredients except ice into blender. Blend until smooth. Add ice and blend on high until smooth and frosty. Pour into pitcher or individual wineglasses. *Makes 4 servings (1 quart).*

Calories 120

✳ Mexican Coffee ✳

Here's a terrific way to top off your next dinner party. With this winning combination of coffee, chocolate, and whipping cream, who needs dessert?

Net Carbs 5

> 1½ ounces coffee liqueur
>   (page 59)
> 5   ounces hot black coffee
> Light whipped topping
> Sugar-free (or low-carb) semi-
>   sweet chocolate, shaved

Pour coffee liqueur into coffee mug. Add coffee. Top with 3 tablespoons whipped topping and ½ ounce shaved chocolate.

Calories 150

✴ Orange Liqueur ✴
(Mock Grand Marnier)

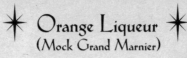

Because Grand Marnier uses a rich cognac base for a wonderful, complex flavor, it's both pricey and loaded with sugar. Here's how to make your own for a fraction of the cost and a fraction of the carbs.*

Net Carbs 3

2　cups cognac (moderately priced like a good V.S.)
1　medium orange
½　cup splenda
2　tablespoons granulated sugar

Pour the cognac into a 2-cup jar with a lid. Using a zester or vegetable peeler, slice several long pieces of orange peel (avoiding white pith) off the orange and place in the jar. Peel the orange and separate the orange sections.

Cut each section lengthwise and place into jar. Add Splenda and sugar. Stir or cover and shake. Let set at room temperature for at least 2 weeks.

Strain the mixture, pressing to release juice. Discard fruit and peel, and strain orange liqueur into a bottle or jar and cover. Keeps indefinitely. *Makes 16 1-ounce servings.*

Calories 75

*Substituting Mock Grand Marnier for any recipe in this book that calls for Grand Marnier will save you an *additional* 2 carbs for each ½-ounce used in the recipe.

✳ Sangria ✳

Red wine and fresh fruit blend together to make a beautiful display in this refreshing and easy-to-make Spanish libation. Place several pitchers on a buffet table and watch how fast it disappears!

Net Carbs 4*

1	bottle (750 milliliters) red wine (such as a moderately priced cabernet or Spanish rioja)
4	ounces brandy
½	cup orange juice
2	tablespoons lemon juice
2	tablespoons Splenda Granular
½	teaspoon orange extract
1	orange, sliced thin
1	lemon, sliced thin
2	cups sugar-free (diet) ginger ale

Pour wine and brandy into a large glass serving pitcher. Add fruit juices, Splenda, and orange extract. Stir. Push fruit slices down into wine mixture. (Stop here if you're not serving the Sangria right away, the mixture will keep for several hours.) Just prior to serving, add ginger ale. Stir briefly. To serve, pour 6 ounces into ice-filled collins glass. (To serve buffet style, add ice to pitcher before serving.) *Makes 9 servings.*

Calories 100

*does not include eating fruit

✳ Superb Orange & Brandy Coffee ✳

You'll find a nonalcoholic version of this delicious orange-scented coffee in Marlene's book *Fantastic Food with Splenda*. Here, the addition of brandy makes it even better!

Net Carbs 3

6	tablespoons ground coffee
1	small orange
3	tablespoons Splenda Granular
2	teaspoons honey
4	cups water
9	ounces brandy

Place coffee in filter. Grate peel of orange into grounds. Measure Splenda and honey directly into the empty coffeepot. Brew coffee using 4 cups of water. Add brandy to pot or place 1½ ounces of brandy in each of 6 coffee mugs; add coffee and serve. *Makes 6 servings.*

Calories 110

Variation: Nonalcoholic variation: eliminate brandy—makes 5 servings, each with 4 grams net carbs.

Novelties

✳ Chuck Wagon ✳

Until now only our family and friends have had the privilege of enjoying this perfectly perfected premium Sidecar. Now you can too.

Net Carbs 4

½ **ounce B&B**
½ **ounce vodka**
½ **ounce cognac**
½ **ounce lemon juice**
2–3 drops orange extract
Orange twist

Pour all ingredients except for orange twist into a shaker ¾ full of ice. Shake well. Strain into a chilled cocktail glass. Garnish with orange twist.

Calories 120

✳ Cognac Martini ✳

Served very cold rather than warmed, cognac produces a terrific postmeal martini. It is the perfect complement to a fine cigar, if you are so inclined.

Net Carbs 0

3 ounces cognac
1 lemon twist

Pour cognac into a shaker ⅔ full of ice. Shake well. Strain into a chilled martini glass. Run lemon twist around rim before dropping into glass.

Calories 195

✳ Frozen Coffee Cocktail ✳

Our version of the coffeehouse favorite
is guaranteed to give you a jolt!

**Net
Carbs
7**

1	tablespoon hot water
1	tablespoon Splenda
1	teaspoon instant coffee granules
1	ounce half-and-half
2	ounces coffee liqueur (page 59)
1	cup crushed ice

Pour all ingredients into blender. Blend on high until
smooth. Pour into a tall collins glass.

Calories 140

✦ Ginger Snap ✦

Not quite a cookie, but definitely full of snap!

Net Carbs 0

2 ounces brandy (or blended Canadian whiskey)
½ teaspoon Splenda Granular
Diet ginger ale
Orange slice

Pour brandy into a tall collins glass. Add Splenda. Stir. Top with diet ginger ale. Garnish edge with orange slice.

Calories 130

✳ Jell-O Shooters ✳

Here's a way to put fewer calories and more jiggle into this favorite Jell-O treat. Serving options include using 2-ounce disposable cups, like the college crowd does, or stacking jelled cubes into small cordial glasses, like upscale bars do. Either way, these say "Party!"

Net Carbs 0

1 small box (4-serving size) sugar-free Jell-O
1 cup boiling water
1 cup vodka or rum*

Dissolve Jell-O in boiling water, stirring very well. Add liquor. Pour into either disposable cups, small-cubed ice cube trays, or a rectangular pan. Chill until set. If panned, cut Jell-O into small cubes. Serve as desired. *Makes 8 2-ounce servings.*

Calories 50

Variations: The variations of flavored gelatin and liquor combinations are endless, but here are a few ideas to get you started in experimenting on your own:

* **Mad Orange Shooter**—orange-flavored Jell-O with Mandarin Orange vodka
* **Sunshine Shooter**—lemon Jell-O with Citron vodka
* **Tropical Shooter**—strawberry-banana Jell-O with rum

*For firmer gelatin, use only ¾ cup alcohol

✳ Lemon Drop ✳

Trendy drinks come and go, but we think this current hit is a definite keeper. With the great sweet-and-sour taste of the popular candy that gives this cocktail its name, here's one guaranteed to make you smile.

Net Carbs 4

Lemon twist
½ teaspoon sugar (optional)*
1½ ounces Citron vodka
½ ounce lemon juice
2 teaspoons Splenda Granular

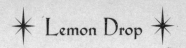

Wet lemon twist with a couple of drops of lemon juice. Run around rim of chilled cocktail glass. Holding glass horizontally over a plate, sprinkle sugar around rim. Pour vodka, lemon juice, and Splenda into a shaker ⅔ full of ice. Shake. Strain into the sugar-rimmed glass. Add twist.

Calories 110

*If you omit the sugar-rimmed glass, subtract 2 grams net carb.

✳ Ultra-Low-Carb Lemon Drop ✳

With only 1 gram of carbohydrate and a
mere 100 calories, this is truly a treat.

**Net
Carbs
1**

> 1½ **ounces citron vodka**
> 1½ **teaspoons Splenda**
>   **Granular**
> ¼   **teaspoon lemon extract**
> **Lemon twist**

Pour all ingredients except lemon twist into a shaker
⅔ full of ice. Shake well. Strain into a chilled cocktail
glass. Add twist.

Calories 100

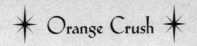# ✳ Orange Crush ✳

Blushing with gorgeous orange color and bursting with intense orange flavor, this drink looks as good as it tastes.

Net Carbs 0

> 1½ ounces Mandarin Orange (or other orange-flavored) vodka
> 5 ounces diet orange soda
> Thin orange slice*

Fill a tall collins glass with crushed ice. Pour vodka and soda into glass. Stir lightly. Garnish rim with orange slice.

Calories 100

*Add 1.5 grams carbohydrate if you eat the orange slice.

✳ Saketini ✳

East meets West in this Asian-inspired martini made with a touch of sake (rice wine). Try it with your favorite Asian meal or sushi.

Net Carbs 1

3	**ounces Ketel One or other high-quality vodka**
½	**ounce sake**
	Lemon twist

Pour vodka and sake in shaker ⅔ full of ice. Shake very well. Strain into chilled cocktail glass. Rim lemon twist around edge of glass and drop into drink

Calories 200

✳ Vanilla Velvet ✳

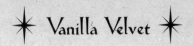

Sweet and silky, this alcoholic version of a vanilla crème is oh, so soothing. Mmm ...

Net Carbs 2

2	ounces vodka
1	ounce light cream
2–3	teaspoons Splenda Granular
¾	teaspoon vanilla extract

Pour all ingredients into a shaker ½ full of ice. Shake. Strain drink into ice-filled rocks glass.

Calories 190

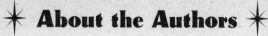 About the Authors

Chuck and Marlene Koch reside in the San Francisco Bay area, where they love to entertain family and friends. Marlene is a bestselling author, nutrition consultant, and professional cooking instructor who specializes in good health and good food. Her fabulous recipes have been featured on the Food Network and the *Today Show* as well as in publications for Atkins Nutritionals, *Cooking Light* magazine, and *Diabetic Cooking* magazine. You can find her on the web at www.marlenekoch.com. Chuck, anointed by all who know him as a "drink master," is widely known for his quality and creativity in making the perfect drink for every menu and occasion.

Illustrator Christopher Dollbaum holds a master's degree in Fine Arts from the University of Washington in Seattle, where he currently resides. He is known for his work in ceramic sculpture as well as his fine drawings.

Also by Marlene Koch

available wherever books are sold